The Kitty Kama Sutra

The Only Sex Manual Your Cat Will Ever Need

The Kitty Kama Sutra

The Only Sex Manual Your Cat Will Ever Need

by Richard Smith

Illustrations by Susann Ferris Jones

Sterling Publishing Co., Inc.
New York

A John Boswell Associates Books

Text Design by Nan Jernigan

Library of Congress Cataloging-in-Publication Data Available

2 4 6 8 10 9 7 5 3 1

Published by Sterling Publishing Co., Inc.
387 Park Avenue South, New York, NY 10016
© 2006 by Sterling Publishing Co.

Distributed in Canada by Sterling Publishing
c/o Canadian Manda Group, 165 Dufferin Street
Toronto, Ontario, Canada M6K 3H6
Distributed in the United Kingdom by
GMC Distribution Services
Castle Place, 166 High Street, Lewes, East Sussex, England BN7 1XU
Distributed in Australia by Capricorn Link (Australia) Pty. Ltd.
P.O. Box 704, Windsor, NSW 2756, Australia

Printed in China
All rights reserved

Sterling ISBN-13:978-1-4027-4136-4
      ISBN-10: 1-4027-4136-7

For information about custom editions, special sales, premium and
corporate purchases, please contact Sterling Special Sales
Department at 800-805-5489 or specialsales@sterlingpub.com.

Raves for the Kitty Kama Sutra
from Actual Users

"Awesome! By the third page we shed our inhibitions and had some good times."

> Socks and Winkle,
> customer service reps, Calcutta

"An outstanding sex manual we wish to tell you. Such naughtiness, woo hoo."

> Zeke and Katrina,
> house cats, Taj Mahal

"No technical jargon. Just frank, tastefully presented pleasure hints that redefine the concept of sweet surrender."

> Rabindranath Tagore,
> sex therapist-in-waiting to the Empress Mingh

"Our bubble baths will never be the same, thanks to Kitty Kama Sutra."

> Buster and Olivier,
> jewelry designers

Table of Contents

Introduction

Kitty sexuality, ever mysterious, flourished throughout India during the Mughlai Period, when the Great Emperor Ghana "Biff" Sag decreed that cats, too, had a right to be amorous and make as much love as his two-legged subjects (dogs throughout the land petitioned but to no avail). This new and improved Kitty Kama Sutra, translated from the original, and updated, codifies feline love behavior, making it easy for even the novice cat to enjoy, with a partner, a rich and spicy sex life. We further promise that those who follow the book carefully will never again call a friend to complain, "All the good cats are taken."

Kitty Kama Sutra

1134

Mishma II, Great-grandfather of Tonda the Tabby, invents "Fragrance of the Orient" kitty litter ("One Sniff and She Is Yours") which, when sat upon, emits super-erotic endorphins, the forerunner to today's Glade Plug-Ins.

1255

Suleyman the Kitty, court cat to Vashti the Majestic, discovers that changing positions during sex prevents bedsores. Is given the Distinguished Service Cross by Mowgli, the Caliph of Mysore.

1377

"Not tonight, dear." Shalimar, a long-haired Persian and concubine to Gandhi, Manx of Kanpur, feigns headache to avoid sex. First instance of pet imitating owner.

1498

Vasco da Gama reaches India, brings along Monroe, his cat, who ravishes every kitty he sees, plus three nightingales. Becomes renowned philosopher and writes definitive paper on frigidity.

1522

Corfu the Siamese discovers that dim lighting during motel trysts not only enhances the mood, but reassures voluptuous cats who fear that the sight of cellulite will turn partner off.

1599

Mittens Galileo, astronomer cat-royal to the Maharajah of Agra and author of *Size Doesn't Matter*, a self-help parchment for under-endowed cats, discovers, during orgasm, that the earth moves. Spends declining years in a loony bin.

1689

Taj Mahal first used as a romantic getaway by cats. Muffin, an American shorthair and his bride take advantage of the off-season rates to spend their honeymoon in the Mogul Suite, where they engage in endless hanky-panky.

Calendar of Love

1726

Cindy, an Egyptian mau, while vacationing in Rangoon, trademarks the love cry *"Koka Shastra, Bingo!"* which means "Don't stop now!" She retires wealthy and becomes a realtor in Beverly Hills.

1867

Definitive study of during-sex mood killers by Simon of Delhi suggests that passion is definitely diminished by the cat who comes to bed wearing over-the-calf tube socks.

1958

Self-pleasuring by cats declared taboo by Whiskers, the Grand Mufti of Tobruk, who claims it causes blindness and vomiting on owner's carpet. Exception made if there's nothing good on TV.

1971

Snuggles, the Chivalrous Cat of Madras, discovers that a good-night kiss on the first date is practically guaranteed if he picks up the dinner check. He applies for and is the first cat to receive an American Express card.

1995

Tabatha, a Pakistani shorthair hangs a DO NOT DISTURB sign outside and is first cat to have sex in a gym bag. Afterward, rolls over and falls asleep under a rhododendron bush.

2005

Blossom and Kukla, the commuting cats of Bombay, make love using the park-and-ride position. They are considered innovators and given the Nobel Prize.

Part I
First Intimacies
The Warming Up of Kitty

Cats are naturally romantic, hence creating a romantic mood is ever so easy. Gadjii, the gynecologist-in-waiting to Kukla, the love goddess of Calcutta, says to anoint the body with rare oils and spice, myrrh, or fennel for a shockingly erotic effect, then heighten the loveliness with a gentle dab of patchouli behind each ear. The Kitty Bhagavad Gita also makes mention of the attractiveness of the cat who wears a flower behind her ear.

Note: *The kitty whose romantic companion is a wicked temptress—a cat in a miniskirt or a Maine Coon with a sultry Burmese—may already be aroused. In that case, you may leap directly to Part III: The Fires of Ranchipur—The Eleven Positions of Love. You have no moments to lose.*

And, to be sure, a come-hither cat look,
used by the tabby-seductress with

bedroom eyes can be greatly enhanced
with the wearing of fishnet stockings.

There is no cat alive able to resist the
Fiery Glance Look of Passion, also
known, in Karachi, as Flashing One's
Lover the High Beams.

The strewing of fragrant rose petals
in the path of the beloved is a
further enticement to pleasure,

but to eat them is bad karma.

And what better way to rinse away the stress of catching mice, or napping, than a bubble bath together. Surround the tub with bath candles then, as you and your partner sip vintage sweet cream from champagne flutes, gently and suggestively

wash each other with a fish-shaped loofah (available online from Bhel Poori Imports). Finish the ritual by anointing each other with precious oils stolen from your owner's bath cabinet.

After you have toweled each other off,
further hotness can be achieved by snuggling together and watching mouse porn
with Sanskrit subtitles.

Let your fevered imaginations run so
wild! These are not the modest little
wretches that hide in the walls. These are
especially recruited Bollywood mice,
renowned for their beauty and tight abs.
Observe and learn things.

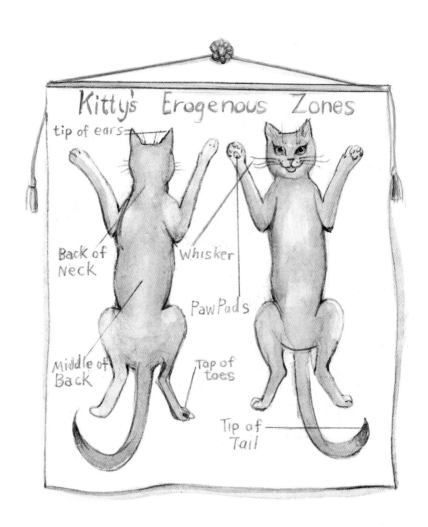

Sexually sensitive areas vary with each partner. With one kitty, it may be under her chin, with another whose hearing is keen, the tips of the ears. Don't be afraid to experiment until you get it very correctly.

The Lusty Temptress Meowing Activity

The language of love is, indeed, seductive, and the kitty who woos his partner by meowing a sonnet ("Ode to My Beloved Krishna" has been used with much success). can, to be sure, write his own ticket. Additionally, we humbly offer the Seven Murmurs of Dondi to whisper in the ear of your beloved:

"Call me a tiger, it gets me excited."

"Have you heard anything about the weather?"

"Hurry, my owner will be home soon."

"I desire you this moment, thy whiskers are so manly."

"I like to be tied up."

25

Amplify the now-happening arousal
feeling with the secret Fur Tussling Ritual
of Omar, The Skateboarding Cat of
Hindustan.

The kitty with a lovely singing voice may wish to serenade his lover with a well-chosen song, accompanying himself on the sitar. (Known in the Kama Sutra as the Maharishi Billy Joel Musical Benefits Package.)

But . . . the cat with a less than melodious singing voice (the Hoarse Cat of Ramar, for instance) may choose merely to play romantic music. If you put on Cole Porter and dance whisker-to-whisker things will not cool down we assure you.

Even better, the musical cat who can strum
"Memories" on the ukulele, will melt even
the coldest cat.

In addition to the the Bombay Belle
High-Quality Earlobe Lick, many cats
find the noise of their partner's heavy
breathing a turn-on, unless partner
somehow ruins the mood with bad breath.
A brief time-out for a gargle with oolong
tea will remedy such thing.

Ask yourself, lovers: Is now not a good
time for the forbidden pleasures Dashiki
Nose Bite so favored by the Indian
romance guru Biryani Gitlitz? It will sure
make your partner your love slave.

Follow such activity with the tuna fondle.
Do you hear the purring? Is it musical?
Like Ravi Shankar playing his harmonica?
Good. It means sure-fire arousal . . . and
you are ready for the Pratha Galosh
Hurricane of Mouth Kisses that allow you
to pleasure each other with vigor. Between
kisses, sips from a cup of purified, environ-
mentally safe water from the Ganges
permit the renewal of strength.

Note: *Be gentle, whisker burn is not a pleasant
thing, especially if you must appear at work the
next day.*

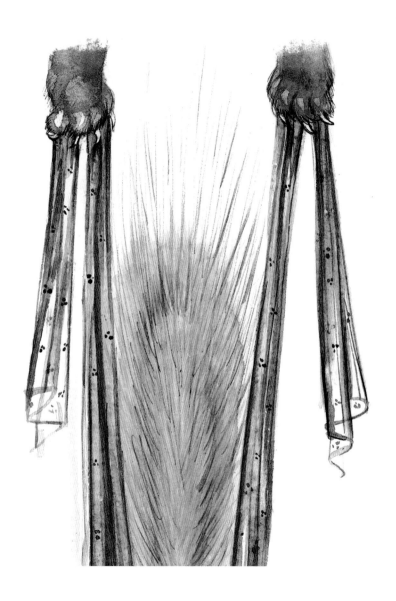

Oops! Too much passion. The curse of the dreaded sari wedgie. . .

Part II — Fur Play
(Much like foreplay, except with an abundance of giggling.)

We now advance to new and extra-glorious intimacies. Rubbing against each other while whispering sweet endearments can set that sensual mood so beloved by roguish alley cats. The tongue-tied kitty may wish to avail himself of the number one favorite of Ali, the editorial director of the Kama Sutra:

> "Madam, I wish you to be the mother of my children."

> This will cause a lover to vibrate with joy.

When muttering such sweet nothings into the partner's ear, let us not forget the fragrant power of tuna breath…

or, for Israeli cats. . . lox breath.

Words are lovely, but deeds are better. It is at this present moment that the special Hindu Kush fondle will excite the kitty who is sensitive and ticklish.

Did you know, wise lovers, that the average cat has 422 erogenous zones, including:

- The tip of the tail

- Those darling little ears

- The forehead (make her yours with the Caress of Ottoman)

- Her feeding dish

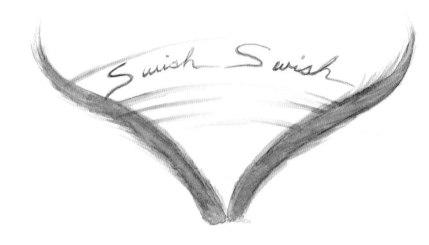

Is now a good time to start the petting-below-the-waist moves that ancient cats used to make their partner so excited? Why, of course. If you see kitty's tail go swish-swish, you are on the right track.

Are your caresses producing sounds of bliss (the Jubilee of Happy Meows, alluded to by Dondi in the Cha Cha Pindi Book of Writhing)? No? Then check: Have you retracted your claws?

Do not stop now . . . is not kitty's heart beating faster? Is passion causing her ticks to blush? Prepare, oh lovers. Wonderment is just beginning.

Be aware that a cat appreciates the partner who is an animal in bed, causing the fur to do things that fur was never meant to do.

Is kitty a bit deviant? So many modern cats are. Here (for demonstration purposes only) our dominatrix, dressed as Little Red Riding Hood, uses her tail to give her lover a Backlash. Yes, it is good to be adventurous.

Note: *The Kama Sutra strictly forbids bondage; cats hate authority.*

Are kitty's eyes crossed? Yes? This is a
for-sure indicator of unspeakable joy.

Erotic fantasies play a significant role in heightening the mysterious lovemaking experience:

The Official Kitty Kama Sutra Rating Scale:

1. We are on a deserted island with a glorious beach. As we make love, a magical cat-genie named Irving, wearing a turban and flowing toga, feeds us herring and goldfish to keep our strength up. 🐾🐾🐾🐾🐾

2. We are on our honeymoon. We have the luxury suite at the local ASPCA, which includes valet parking and a Jacuzzi in which we luxuriate, NAKED!! sipping buttermilk and exchanging secret meows. 🐾🐾🐾🐾

3. We both "accidentally" brush against our owner's leg, which, as luck would have it, is clad in corduroy (wide wale). The rubbing motion so excites us that, after ordering owner from the room, we ravish each other on the oriental rug. 🐾🐾🐾🐾🐾

4. I am lying in the kitchen, dozing in a pool of sunlight when, suddenly, a masked cat wearing a Zorro hat jumps in through the open window. I protest that, "I'm not that kind of cat." He ignores me and proceeds to do things to my furry body that make me change my mind. Afterward, we share a large piece of gefilte fish that was left on the kitchen table. 🐾🐾🐾

5. While sharing a mouse at an upscale restaurant, my lover reaches under the table and, her eyes gleaming, begins to grope me. She does it so well, so consummately, that I feel the earth move. We get disgracefully turned on, skip dessert, hail a cab, and spend the rest of the night making fiery love in a warm Dumpster. 🐾🐾🐾🐾

You must now tell your lover what gets you truly excited. If he runs screaming from the room. . .

or curls up in a little ball and starts to suck his thumb, get another cat.

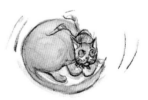

Kama Sutra Love Wisdom

How do you know when your lover is in the mood?

Heavy breathing?

Giving the nanny the night off?

The six signs that your lover is ready for Aloo Baigan:

1. He begins to kiss your neck.

2. He then blows in your ear.

3. He nibbles the tip of your nose.

4. He administers gentle love bites to your tail.

5. He pulls the shades.

6. He tell his assistant to hold all calls.

Now we are ready for the Garlic-Naan
intimate entwining of whiskers, which,
when achieved, means you are either
engaged, or tangled up and must seek
assistance from the dog.

Are you now, sweet lovers, prepared for the ecstasies of
Pakistan? Not sure? Then see our exclusive Kama Sutra
Ready or Not Checklist™ to help you decide.

✓ You both are tingling ____
✓ Your fur is extra-lustrous ____
✓ Your frenzied purrs are drowning out
   your owner's snoring ____
✓ You're meowing sweet nothings into
   each other's ear _____
✓ You've stopped listening to your iPod ____
✓ The dog is at the neighbors ____
✓ You can't stop pouncing on each other ____
✓ Your excitement is causing you both to ferment ____

All set? Then let us proceed to. . .

Part III —
The Fires of Ranchipur —
The Eleven Positions of Kitty Love

The nearly limitless variety of kitty positions was first explored by Hadji Ben Singh in his highly regarded Sexual Code of Spike, which lists 11,688 positions! Including the seldom-attempted Yaso-Samosa, in which the two lovers engage in a threesome with a goat.

Before commencing to make perfervid love it is good, however, to decide: your place or his? Many cats, when seized by the *Demon Goddess of Wildness*, settle for anywhere: the patio, an intimate alley or, if they like to be watched, next to a mouse hole. Some helpful Kama Sutra–type suggestions:

At Your Place	At His Place
You're more in control, you *know* the sheets are clean, and you have, if you get hungry, great snacks in the fridge.	You're taking a huge chance on the amenities. Instead of clean sheets, he may just flip the old ones over. In the fridge, at best, a six-pack and half jar of herring in wine sauce.
You get to choose the mood music.	His CD player may be covered by empty pizza boxes.
You live alone.	He may have a surprise roommate (like his mother).
May be difficult to get him to leave if you seek morning privacy.	You can leave if his morning cough gets on your nerves.
You keep a photo of your favorite vet on your night-stand for luck.	He keeps a photo of his ex on his nightstand ("We're just friends").

If you have done your special Keema Naan stretching exercises, you are now ready to engage in actual positions. Note: Varying the positions will prevent the kitty-lovers from:

1. Growing bored
2. Fermenting

1. The Lotus

Here we have the kitty on top and the lotus on the bottom. A particularly wonderful position for the cat who seeks, during lovemaking, to commune with nature.

2. The Reverse Lotus

Here we have the Shrimp Scampi Biryani
Variation, in which the lotus is on top and
kitty is torturing the hamster.

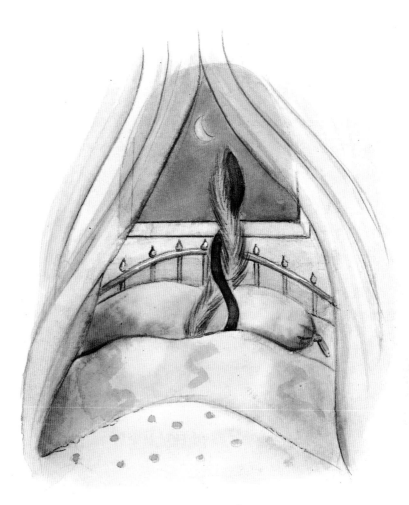

3. Sen Sen Interwoven Tails

Kitties who experience first-time jitters
(and what cat doesn't?) can enjoy this
position, which is intimate, yet not
overly so. An especially promising position for cats on their wedding night.

4. *The Garden of Earthly Delights*

Both kitties intertwine and float blissfully on a sea of tranquility. (Releases the "healing" energies so sought after by cats.

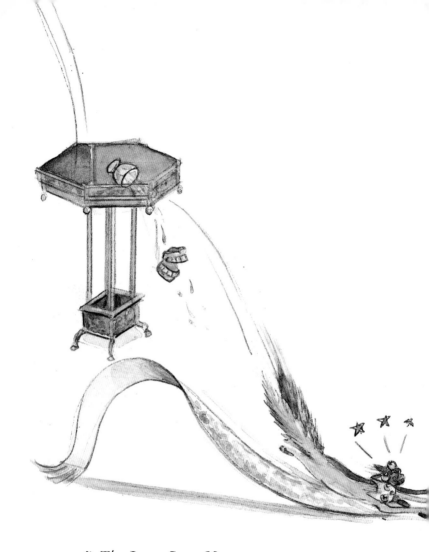

5. The Jump-Leap Maneuver:
This special high-energy love position, if executed correctly, will knock over either a very expensive vase or the glass containing your owner's teeth. Oh-oh, watch out for rug burn.

Kama Sutra Love Wisdom

Nervous about those few extra pounds, oh dear voluptuous kitty? Don't be.

1. You carry them well.
2. They'll come in handy if you're on the bottom.
3. Most cats look thinner when they're lying down.

Be assured, no matter what you weigh, that your lover really wants you for your mind (and, perhaps, your health insurance).

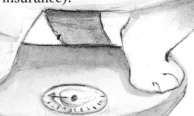

6. Birdsong at Morning
A romantic favorite in which both kitties, after removing the bird, enjoy intimacy in their very own love nest. (The preferred activity for outdoorsy cats.)

7. The "Quickie"
This position is for the kitties who either:
Expect their owner back at any moment; or
Are on their lunch hour.

8. Back-to-Back

Admittedly, this position pushes the frontiers of sex, but for very shy lovers who, during intimacy, prefer to stare out the window, this is just the ticket. (Not recommended if male partner circumcized.)

9. The Missionary
This is, of course, the standard position,
first recorded in the Bamba Treatise on the
Intoxication of Good Lovemaking. This is
an ideal position for the kitties who,
during sex, wish to groom each other.

10. Riding the Kitty

Here the submissive cat gives his partner a piggyback ride, enabling the "rider" to conserve energy and feel pampered. (Do not be distracted by the yipping Pomeranian.)

Note: *It is a very egotistical cat who, during moments of super passion, calls out his own name:*

> *"Mittens, Oh Lord, Mittens."*

11. Standing Up (the Blitzma Rondo)
Standing up, facing each other, is an
ancient and favorite position of cats
who are of equal height. Gaze into each
other's eyes and meow words of love.
(Best done in front of a mirror, unless,
on Match.com, male cat lied about his
height).

Kama Sutra Love
Wisdom

During extra-steamy love-
making, make switching
positions a snap by grasping
your partner's love handles.

Did the moment of Supreme Ecstasy not
send shivers down your spine?
Is the earth not moving,
oh joyous kitties?

*Do you not hear trumpets
blow?
The ocean swell?*

Are your two hearts beating as one?
If not, ask for your money back.
We will not be offended.

Part IV—
After the Good Time: The Cuddly Post-Lovemaking Activities

See, oh languorous cats, you didn't need to watch that better-sex video after all. Snuggling and holding each other close while murmuring the sweet purrs of love found in the Gandhi-Mitzvah section of *Tantric Sex for Pleasure and Profit* will add to that feeling of closeness, unless one partner is trying to see the time.

Here is the perfect moment to lavish
extreme praise on the lover who satisfied
your every desire (two or three meows
should do it).

Some cats relax after sex by lighting a cigarette.

A word of caution: The male partner who, instead of stroking his partner and expressing his love, merely rolls over and falls asleep will not win mulligatawny points. Especially if his partner is lying there, staring at the ceiling, wondering, is that all there is? and listening to him snore.

But, if you are both exhibiting the

Cloud 9 Staring Into Space
Expression of Wondrousness®

then your happiness is sublime.

Let your body language proclaim the excellence of your lover by:

◆ Spooning
◆ Snuggling
◆ Cuddling
◆ Playful pouncing

You will lie there, in each other's arms,
displaying a shocking indifference to:

◆ Fish farming
◆ Illegal immigration
◆ Seducing our trade deficit
◆ Your guests waiting downstairs

Did you know, dear kitties, that Kra Dashiki, the love expert of Bingsoor, says that nestling against each other and dozing can take the place of meaningful conversation?

The Post-Lovemaking Afterglow —
What are they thinking?

Breed	Comments
Maine Coon	Can he tell I was faking?
Persian	I wonder, was it good for her?
Russian Blue	I wonder, was it good for me?
Siamese	Wow, I never did that with my ex.
Scottish Fold	That was such a good career move.
Angora	That's the most fun I ever had with my clothes off.
Ragdoll	Oops, I think I pulled something.
Sphynx	Oooooooooooooooooom mmmmmmm.

Time for some kitty pillow talk. Take a rest from the monsoon of caresses and mutter some things to say, like:

- "What have you told your friends about me?"
- "Have to go put money in the meter."
- "I hope we produced a male heir."
- "Must go, my owner expects me home."
- "I'll call you."
- "You just lie there and look beautiful, I'll go steal us some salmon croquettes."
- "Where is this relationship going?"

And do not forget: It is the kitty who did the most work during lovemaking who is entitled to breakfast in bed.

Appendix: Secrets of the Orient

Secrets of the Orient # 1
Perfuming the Breath with Aphrodisiacs

The Kama's favorite during-sex munchies include:

> Tuna tidbits

> Animal crackers (guess which shape are kitty's favorites)

> Altoids

> Beef lips

> Moon pies
> (truly a reliable libido
> expander)

> Salmon (wild only)

> Glazed mice (go easy on the curry)

> The palate-captivating basmati liver (especially good if cooked with a killer mango powder).

Secrets of the Orient # 2
Focusing on theAct of Love

The passionate kitty must cleanse the mind of
intrusive thoughts that can detract from the joys
of sex. Some typical "bad karma" cat thoughts include:

Hurry, we have theater tickets.

Am I making too much noise?

Am I satisfying my partner? And if so,
why is she in the other room?

Is my partner satisfying me? And if so,
why am I obsessing about (yum) anchovies?

I wish this Maine coon cat would change
position, my leg is falling asleep.

Can I get away with wearing the same outfit to
work tomorrow?

Secrets of the Orient # 3
How to Read Your Lover's Paw

Each spot on your lover's paw will illicit the following responses.

Point 1.	I'm passionate about little ear nibbles.
Point 2.	Do not stop, oh my Tandoori Tiger.
Point 3.	I make a swoon when you press me here.
Point 4.	Loud moans of pleasure.
Point 5.	Sshhhh, our fleas will hear us.

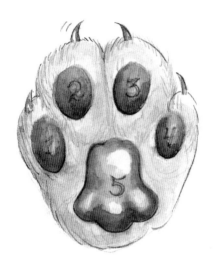

Secrets of the Orient #4
De-Coding the Rapturous Tail Swish

1. "Oh, oh, my cherished Dervish, this is soooooooooooo good."

2. "A little to the left, you wondrous brute."

3. "Not tonight, dearest, I have fleas."

4. "Ravish me further, oh Gypsy Hero of the Ganges."

5. "Have you heard anything about the weather?"

6. "Love your French maid outfit."

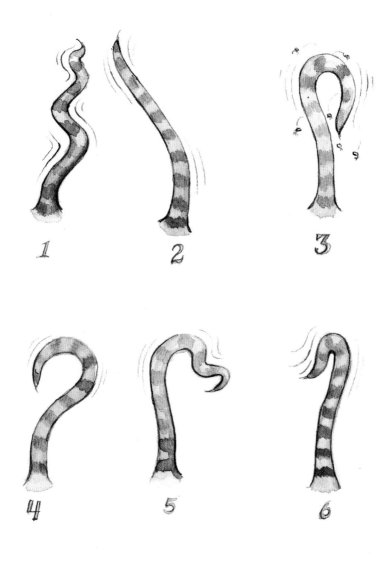

1   2   3

4   5   6

Secrets of the Orient # 5
What to Wear

What to wear during the lovemaking act? Except for a welding mask, the old Kama Sutra made little mention of the many unusual outfits that could make a cat feel "special," even a bit risqué. Modern cats, however, especially the deranged ones, have several favorite outfits:

- Latex jumpsuit
- Batman outfit
- Leg irons
- A veil (for the cat who seeks mystery)
- Just a little bell around the neck

Kama Sutra Memories

Please take a moment, dear lovers to record the joyousness of your activities.

How many times did you do it? _____

Who kept count?   He did_____   She did_____
        The parrot_____   The vet_____

Arousal initiated by: Blowing in partner's ear___
        Making eyes at partner_____
        Reading poetry_____Grooming each other_____
        Terrorizing the dog_____

Favorite place for lovemaking: Rug_____
        Patio_____   Limo_____   Owner's lap_____

Most sensitive erogenous zone: Tail_____
        Side of face_____   My dish_____

Things to be happy about after this incredible night of
love: I'm so relaxed___
        I love my partner even more___

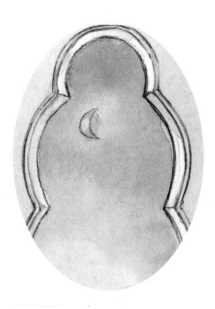